For Sue

THE CINNAMON OF DESIRE

_with thanks for all
your kindnesses & friendship_

poems by

Jay S. Carson

MAIN STREET RAG PUBLISHING COMPANY
CHARLOTTE, NORTH CAROLINA

Library of Congress Control Number: 2012953876

ISBN: 978-1-59948-394-8

Produced in the United States of America

Main Street Rag
PO Box 690100
Charlotte, NC 28227
www.MainStreetRag.com

For my family and friends
whose love and support
made these poems possible.

Acknowledgements

Thanks to the following journals where these poems first appeared.

Along These Rivers and *Euphony*: "Baking the Ginger Boy's Tongue"
California Quarterly: "Announcing November"
Cape Rock: "Wounded Year"
Confluence: "Physics for Real Life"
Connecticut Review: "Haiti Well," "Haiti Ill"
Eclipse: "Communion"
Epicenter: "When Finishing That Excellent . . . Lamb"
Fission of Form: "Shrouded"
Folio: "White Hot Justice"
Fourth River: "Sects"
G.W. Review: "Pomme de Terre"
Hawaii Review: "How I Would Become a Blacksmith"
Lullwater Review: "Things My Father Taught Me"
Mudfish: "Creative Writing 909"
Natural Language: "Sonnet by Guide Dog"
Paper Street: "Jay Bird," "Shame"
Pearl: "Richard Nixon and Me"
Pittsburgh City Paper: "Something in the Eye"
Pittsburgh Post-Gazette: "Collected on Penn"
RiverSedge: "Lights Out in Miracle City," "Minnesota Sweet"
Rune: "Memento Mori," "Dead Cat"
Sanskrit: "The Garden of Lost Girlfriends"
Soundings East: "Hemispheres"
Studio One: "Another American Childhood"
Wisconsin Review: "The Bells of Rhymney"

CONTENTS

I

None of us can forgive our families for not being perfect.
William Faulkner

Regret, acknowledged or not, is the inevitable and in some sense necessary context—the bedrock—of all human thought and activity.
Hayden Carruth

BAKING THE GINGER BOY'S TONGUE

What do you want?
The white uniformed voice feeds
my anxious sweet hunger, but iced
with the fear of women's words.

"Them, the ones next to," I said.
Crumb buns? You want crumb buns?
Or the flop overs, which? Her voice, knife sharp
as the red nail of her finger stabbing at the cakes.

Her ruffled pink collar, an old
poisoned plain for her mountain head;
a bumpy nose more sure than Sister Pancratious
smelling out my neck and side sweat.

But my brother warned me
of the rancid taste in feminine scented,
sweet words. And how to lower
to Bogart's lip and tongue swagger.

I can't give you any until you say.
Her eyes bulge at me,
like muffins rising in the tin.
Finally, timed and done, I rise.

"Crumb buns, crumb buns,"
I cry quickly, through slitted mouth,
cut open for the first of many times,
by the cinnamon of desire.

JOHN ALDEN WAS A PILGRIM

my father started a 6th grade essay.
Too Abrupt, his teacher wrote
in red ink on the paper and his brain.

Nobody was around to so clearly
mark up my mistakes when
I started my pilgrimage

to my father's liquor cabinet
or medicine chest, wallet.
Not that I was looking for guidance.

Church was boring;
I thought Jesus might be too
intolerant of folks like me

*Hey, those money changers were
just doing a job of work,*
my local gas station owner said.

I thought so too when I slipped away
from a car inspection and helped myself
to a few twenties from his till.

When I was jonesing from gin,
there was no Christian bank,
and Jesus didn't care.

Until he did. I got sober;
for me, then, like raising the dead,
but now, as if it were written long ago.

Twenty years after my father was rebuked,
Ernest Hemingway started his first, best novel,
Robert Cohn was middleweight boxing champion at Princeton.

ANOTHER AMERICAN CHILDHOOD

None of us were able to kill Dad,
although we did our damnedest.
My brother was the most obvious
going after the old man
with Marine ready fists.
Mother, more subtle, drinking her way
through his heart and into her sick bed
and an early grave. That almost got him.

At first, I just worked on disappointing him.
You know how football players are ruined
by repeated head injuries. Same principle.

Later, after he fell down a pair of steps, drunk,
I told him he didn't need to go
to the hospital for that nasty old stiffness
that turned out to be a slightly broken neck.

But Dad survived. You could say won.
After all, he mixed the drinks for everybody.
And made my brother agonize guiltily till he died young.
And here he is, now, stabbing
this pen point into my eye for breaking
the Fifth Commandment.

THINGS MY FATHER TAUGHT ME

To play bridge and chess
over whiskey and rotting cheese,
always knowing I would lose.
To never buy on margin.
To wear a blazer at dinner
when old enough to eat with him.
To say, *Let's skip it,*
to the most important things.

To read. To talk in a breeze,
as if nothing mattered
but a big, witty, forgetful brain,
except for its thin-wire razor
for cutting the heart out
of another cortex. To say,
Let's get the hell out of here,
until I have never
been anywhere.

PHYSICS FOR REAL LIFE

No action at a distance, the physicists say.
Only those things that connect, like a slap,
can have a causal relation.

I am two wives, thirty years, a child,
and twenty moving violations away from my
last slap, delivered by Wizard Mom,

who has never really touched me.
I rub my cheek in wonder as she continues
to defy the known laws of physics, reaching

out through six earth feet and a cemetery wall,
past ninety city blocks into my locked redoubt,
smearing everywhere her grey ash of guilt.

DANCING SCHOOL

When she saw me in my suit for dancing school,
my mother called me a new angel. I felt like a fool.
But I went, knowing I had to learn, like to fight.

The girls were all sisterly giggles
and oh-so-circular beginning breasts
and party-dressed legs going
I couldn't imagine where.
And I was to dance with one
whose languid eyes were my first
urge at that tart fruit.

It was just us on that dance floor,
surrounded by furrowed, but jeering faces,
relieved, laughing, scornful mouths.

Those looks, with me still,
started my pull from her;
then, her perfume became sickly sweet,
and I bolted like a released sparrow,
leaving her on that circle of parquet.
I would see that flat beak-line grimace
thirty years later on my abandoned wife.

I have whored plenty since then, following
where the legs went, pushing them, mouths, and asses,
sometimes saying, "C'mon on, mama, c'mon on,"
like they owe me some blood love.
I left my last girlfriend before breakfast,
her hands warming an egg in its perfect shell.

My three-year-old grandson likes oldies,
Dancing on the hardwood living room floor, he sings
in a bird chick voice; his favorite comes through
his gyrations, as his arms flap to the shoulder wings,
"I fell down in a burning ring of fire,
down, down, down . . . ".

MOTHER'S DAYS

The last time I saw him, he was lying drunk
on the floor of the Holy Mary Mother of God Club,
my mother said of a just-elected politician.

I never thought of her as so incisively witty
until I started to drink with her.

Much younger, I learned
to avoid interrupting
her long afternoon hangover sleeps.

If you could walk with me
hobbling around that house
so not to wake angry that ecstasy,

you would know why I prayed so long
through my endless marriages
for warmth, even a purgatory kind.

Or maybe I'm just blind to myself.

I think you have yellow jaundice,
the Chinese intern once told my mother,
and she replied: *How would you know?*

COLLECTED ON PENN

We were a legal 33 together,
but only a pure 11 each, facing
decade by decade, promise before experience,
the way Whitfield lay before Negley, before Aiken,
as we looked up to the top of Penn Avenue,
bright cafés like landing lights,

when the church was called East Liberty Presbyterian
by enough grey-jacketed Protestants,
but dubbed Mellon's Fire Escape by the Catholic
school boys whose fathers had built it.

Eddy had cat his collar up and now
rolled his shoulders to brush it against
the back of his neck, rebalancing
on the peaked stone edge of the church lawn.

We were early for the evening movie
at the Regent, and no one wanted us
stone-smelling kids, the way no one
would want East Liberty
thirty years later.

Bullnecked, smiling Sal
was most open about the wine,
right on the Avenue, pulling it
out of his coat like a sword,
choking its neck.
Put it back; put it back,
two new arrivals said.
We weren't ready.

Past Woolworth's, Murphy's, across
to the Cameraphone, down to Bolans;
and so we walked, tracing, retracing.

We massed at the cashier's booth
like a good small army
as much for bravado as confusion:
Sal and I tactically bought two tickets,
and all five of us were in

Next weekend, we sneak in again
afraid to open the wine,
and open it, and drink,
not daring to answer
the question the nosey cashier
asks: *Why aren't you at home?*

We're ready now.

This is our home.

RAINY DAY RHETORIC

Dark sheets of rain hiss
down Kentucky Avenue,
"Cicero, sunny Cicero."
My father will read
from a splitting leather volume:
him to me, "to lighten today,"
to enjoy the superb stylist,
recto, verso, Latin, English,
transliteration over clouding sherry.

I cannot understand
how to listen to
the rain killing me
in the master's amplified style.

PURGATORY EDUCATION

I was a hoodlum in those days.
Like all kids, I learned
the slim profit margin
of being good outside.

At Sacred Heart Grade School
it paid to keep your heart and mouth shut
or even say something wrong instead of "smart."
Sister's throw of a four-pound paper cutter
at Kenny Kavenaugh's head missed by inches.

At home, food and Coca-Cola
flowed like the whiskey
if you didn't bother the man or woman
involved in their own show
trial of Joe McCarthy justice.

At first, outside, I ran
from the Laramer Avenue gang
and their fists and rocks and pipes.
Through alleys, ducked
into stores, ached to join.

I learned enough abuse
for respect: pushing just
far enough on the just weak enough
to make the crew laugh over stolen beer.

Later, I only hot-wired two cars,
And stole not much money; broke, entered
and wrecked one marriage, maybe
two women, a stomach, liver, heart.

Then I ran from dying,
learned the elixirs of work, others,
and that pesky Nazarene carpenter.

But I still have my favorite memory:
Kenny again, doing perfect hook shots
of pretzel rods through a drugstore side wall fan,
spraying salty brown shavings all over the prescriptions,
getting caught, never crying over the beating.

GOOD FRIDAY

That smoky spring morning
reminded me of fall,
heartbreaking in its promise
and surety of end.
It was Good Friday.
Before Jesus' inheritance,
when it was all on the come:

his bet and belief way back then
and mine that it would be ok, even though
I was nineteen and mostly wondering
the oxygen of women
and why my miracles
always tasted of bourbon.

One latest busy question:
why stop at red lights?

I dealt the traffic tickets in a semicircle
on my brother's kitchen table
like blasphemous apostles
while he finished
the cigar he had lit at the police station
for our confidence.

Eight stop signs, three stoplights, and
a weak little "too fast for conditions."

Two screaming days later,
I dutifully drove them
and a sack of dollars
out of my parents' house
downtown to the fixer,

my uncle, who got sober
with Blackie Reilly, really.

If you had only come to me sooner.
I date the secretary. Could have
stopped it right there, free.
But now I'll have to deal with the Greek.
And believe me, it will cost.

All that help, and they are all dead:
after the moth flies and the rust corrupts,
we really are all a better family

COMMUNION

At my son's wedding,
from the first pew,
I saw how we come forth
for forgiveness and connection,
together and alone.

At first, I would not watch
as if I stumbled into a confessional,
or my parents' lovemaking;
nothing wrong but time and me.
The cut stone frees angels and me.

How we come to God:
stone dark dressed, jacketed and tied,
frieze of downcast eyes reviewing
cast down days, now within reach.

Hands and heads are foremost,
the tools of pleading somehow detached,
like Cicero's, hung over the Roman Senate
for pleading one case too well.

Our open mouths and praying hands
might tell the story of Aleijandinho,
the Brazilian sculptor, the little leprous
cripple, miraculously making masterpieces
with hammer and chisel strapped to his arms.

SECOND HAND SYSTOLE

There's a three o'clock in the afternoon
in this saddest ventricle of the day,

an empty chamber two hours wide
that opened congenitally

as my father cut out his valentine
wife as poorly as my father's father and his

choice—roughly outlining men like my son
leaving uneven faces

missing—not woman-smelling salt and lavender
or the crusty tease of baked yeasty loaves—

but the lost soft touch of tongue and ear:
mama hearing the unspeakable soothing

until it became a soul's chant
breathe less than the dog-panting chest.

Knife through these generations
cardiac board to nursery

to a home painted once on a heart wall
perfectly all in red.

II

Shall I eat my own flesh, drink my own blood?
Aztec ritual response

The Motorcycle you are working on is always yourself.
Robert Persig,
Zen and the Art of Motorcycle Maintenance

PROPORTION

You must get a sense of proportion,
my father said when, at 12, I wanted
to have two members of the Howe Street gang
arrested for punching me in the face,
and again, later, when I made a fool
of a narrow-minded uncle
at a family gathering.
I tried to convince anyone who would listen
that Lyndon Johnson should be impeached —

A sense of proportion

So, years later, I took
a drawing-the-figure course
from a thoughtful artist who,
when I complained of no talent,
said she had *special methods.*

On a bleak Saturday
I wandered into a paint-spattered
room where nothing looked real:
all was giveaway shabby, except
the seven women at easels,
their laser eyes directing mine
to a platform on which a robed woman
was standing, then removing her belt,
until all those lovely nook and nestle places
fell out, and she was just there.

I hopelessly drew lines
that somehow squiggled this woman.

I pleaded with my teacher
for some of her special methods.

Look, she said.

I started to see how
to do comes from how to see,

the line from the body,
only partly through the eye;

success from greed
to own for a moment even
the smallest part of God's iris.

With the day nearly closed,
my teacher came around to look

If you would only worry less about
nipple placement and more about the line . . . .

MEMORIALS

I inherited from my father a set
of brass bookends, Abraham Lincoln
seated, as at his Memorial.

But his hands have broken off.
It is the image of the great reader,
lawyer, now unable to hold a book.

I've been tough on my father,
but I should tell you about his childhood.
And how his parents left him early.

His mother died when he was seven,
his father when he was seventeen.
He was devastated, my mother said.

I never thought much about his loss,
only the dream he painted of life
at Heath's Run Farm, his mother's stories,

except once, when he was explaining
the importance of very specific wills:
that they must mention household goods,

how his aunts and uncles came into the farmhouse
like Sherman's locusts through Georgia
and flew off with all the paintings and silver.

One of those relatives,
recalling a fair man alone,
took him in summers of his law school,

saying to me years later, *I remember
him in the library, sitting by himself,
not even reading, always looking so sad.*

WHITE HOT JUSTICE

Everybody said my father
was a fine attorney
and he bought me through that childhood.
He worked hard to be mostly
fair with us all, but left a sense
of the imperfection of justice,
I suggest that what you think
is equity is really the Lone Ranger.

When my friends and I went to the whorehouses
on the Hill, we all wanted Billie.
Sometimes the pimp or madam
would have to call her in
and she would show up
in an elegant dress
or what I thought was.
She was so beautiful in her dresses,
and then caramel skin, the first time
I noticed black women's
nipples were so dark.

When she said, *What do you want, honey?*
her shock of strawberry hair
floating over those marmalade words,
I couldn't tell her.
Sure, I was a tough
locker room boy, beered up,
who could say *half and half,*
straight fuck, even dare *around the world.*
But when she asked what
I wanted, I was afraid,
more than of the razor fight
downstairs, of the police
who had already threatened jail,
of the tales of brain-rotting syphilis.

In a dream I wear a wig
the color of my ghostly skin
and pound a mahogany gavel.
I say, unaccountably,
take her to my nursery.
My father stands up
from the jury box,
his eyes now perfectly sure,
Stop this endless show.

JAY BIRD

I am the blue lightning
in the backyard of your mind,
shrieking, pecking the sedate warblers,
a honking insistent reminder.

I circle low and perch in your neglected
backyard: rusty slides and swings,
the red of a first bloody nose,
glimpse of white under Amanda's
plaid jumper. I am your nails
scratching on the faded third-grade blackboard,
flutter of sandpiper running
from attack waves.

I am your beautiful
cobalt terror. I bolt
to the nearby university buildings
and watch the lone dental researcher
slink into the medical lab
to break the doped baboons' teeth
with little heavy hammers,
to make human life better.

DEAD CAT

I drove to an ancient hill
in my city to drop off an old friend
at his house in the windy rain.

In the middle of the street
a lump of lifeless fur
became electric.

Our parting laugh broke
at the hissing, cement-skinning
spin of an old cat dying.

Around and around it screeched
in a short-leashed spin of fury,
twirling, wailing as if fighting itself.

Breathless, we watched
the rage of that passing,
wondering at the energy of end.

Is that spinning, howling,
hissing a hope or clear hatred
of the way we must be, and then not?

How will I be if not in hospital-sheeted,
drugged comfort? Bloody terrified,
untouched by friends and family?

Will I understand finally,
or just hate as I whirl
and hiss my ugly farewell?

Now, I won't drive in windshield-
river rain, since I take it for
the fur of furious death.

CREATIVE WRITING 909

What the fuck's a crocus?
Or a lark and evensong
at vespers?

Do they rhyme with myasthenia gravis,
stark, or nightmares like those
my wife suffers from?

Are they found in the sepulchral
corridors of hospital, the identical
plush coffin interiors of doctors' offices?

I don't know how to attach
"only a delicate gilt
of organdy edge" to this life.

I can't name one thing made of alabaster.

HOW I WOULD BECOME A
BLACKSMITH

The artist's colony is a stone's throw over the mountain,
a skip from the summit. Students as old
as me laugh and do art as pretty as the orchids
at Kentuck Nob, a rough diagonal drive
across Rt. 40, then, the shifting gravel walk.

Inside the gift cottage, an eternal blacksmith
looks through my eyes, slow, deep, insistent.
"We have a visiting artist," he says,
"who made an ornate bone saw based on
old medical books; it cuts through metal or anything."

"My wife has a spa appointment," I say.
"I'll come back to see your forge. Tomorrow!"
His eyes saw through my wire of words
into marrow. "The maker will be gone then."
So I go and hear of burning plans for the hardest things.

Banked fires in my mind's back furnace
smolder, remind me of words unwrought,
songs unsung, stories unsaid, unseen. Undone.
The ancient artist has shown me his own forge,
an open hearth to fire my promise.

To return as a student apprentice. To learn
to build again. "You will take home
something you have made; everybody does."
His eyes see my lock, tumblers akimbo,
waiting for the combination of commitment.

I tell of my metal maker to an artist friend
with a wise and definite touch. How the iron bender's
words still bolt in my mind as limbo's gates
cast after me. "When I was there,"
she said, "he was the alabaster man."

TRAVELLER

I have been practicing dignity:

first, a walk like Yul Brenner,
unconquerable, but not presumptuous.

A voice an octave lower than my own,
used as sparingly as the bullets
of the Audi Murphy's peace pistol.

A style as lean
as film noir, exact
to graciously necessary;

a helpful ear to the good,
fearful retribution to the bad,
spare as Gary Cooper;

a vote as careful
as Clint Eastwood's decision
of who lives, dies.

Unless, I have
 just been voyaging

on the large pontoon boat
I once saw, unaccountably
resting in a Pennsylvania field,
stately, meditative, but unmoving,
without one passenger.

SONNET BY GUIDE DOG

It is my master who is blind,
not me. I see your annoyance
at my stolid, insistent job of clearing
paths and warning. I see also
your fear and hopeless grief.
You foolish people who do not play
and keep saying those sad words,
instead of . . . but you know
our clear, happy, and direct voice.
And your tail movement, those awful dances.
I could better guide you, not among
yourselves, but with us. Meanwhile,
stay away. It's an endless
job, leading you one by one.

III

There are three things which are too wonderful for me. Four which I do not understand: the way of an eagle in the sky, the way of a serpent on a rock, the way of a ship in the middle of the sea, and the way of a man with a maid.
Proverbs, 30:18

Your cracked country lips I still wish to kiss as to be by the strength of your skin.
Bob Dylan, "Ramona"

SOMETHING IN THE EYE

Always my shining safe, after-movie place,
Woolworth's was even more brilliant
in the darkness of January's
late afternoon snow.

Cold numbed, film-full gaze,
I stumbled into the women's department:
rings and their glistening quartz stones
as larcenously luminescent, and high as my eyes.

It stunned from the middle of a careless pile
like my pretty Aunt Ann amidst her sisters.
One shop girl talked to another,
her hair as alluring gold as the rings' settings.

I want that ring . . .
for my mother. "It's too small
for your mother; it's a girl's ring."
My sister, then. I want that ring.

Before I married, my wife
talked me out of watching a Lakers-Celtics game
to pick our china. Her planned hour turned
into three as I brought plate after lustrous plate

for her rejection—until the one
I broke and walked away. It was the day before
the last film we saw as single people:
the one about the empty Hermitage Museum.

LIGHTS OUT IN MIRACLE CITY

I'm out midnight moon-hunting
during this early spring eclipse,
to look beyond the light pollution,
above the tulips that quit
too early in brown surrender.

The doctors seem kind
and brilliant, the way they do.
But we are moving beyond
helping or deserving all the help
we want here at Mayo Clinic.

Where is the miracle, deserved or not,
for my still-young-to-me wife?

Then I see the sky, an ominous
table setting, the black plate
not quite covering the moon's white,
last supper of the gods.

The darkness domes over
even this miracle city;
sky-scrapers now beacon weakly
in a yellow diner-candle light.

Cold May, give me one more
serving, a silver sliver of light.

The black plate slips,
giving back light slowly,
finally to a full moon/star set sky,

but still not as clear
the yellow glow on broad Highway 48
out of this flat Minnesota town.

MINNESOTA SUITE

I look out on Silver Lake,
watch a Canada goose stretch
a white stripe under her bill,
causing the impossibly thin neck
to nearly disappear, then quiver
with a swallow.

Her young feed easily under high eyes,
but constant watch does not
prevent them, fuzz pillow light,
from running away, taking me.
I am pulled over water on their
miraculous little suctioned feet

as my wife must be when
the depression lifts and the next
stage begins: to the market, producing
exhausting dinners for guests;
to me, when we fight; to this
clinic where even nature
is watched, and, restless,
runs away.

MY WAY II

If you are worried about your girlfriend's
sexual fidelity, don't read *Swann's Way.*
It will feather your insecurity,
glide through your confidence,
just as Odette is gradually revealed
to be a courtesan, but the worst is

the elegant, educated, and kind man
gradually realizes and accepts first,
that her favors are more important
than his high values, even friends;
that her infidelity is everywhere;
he pecks through to her bisexuality,
as he molts from a dupe, then,
simple customer, finally,
to a doomed husband.

From Odette's touching lie,
*Would that you had left your heart
instead of your gloves, I would not have
returned it,* to her sleeping with his rival,
he watches her sexual promiscuity soar.

Naïve and imprinting, I heard
the song of my darling say our love
flies free; and then the quiet echo
of one of a flock of old customers,
as Odette circles the Paris Bois,
her regular Sunday victory lap, *I slept
with her the night McMann resigned.*

SPRING FISHING

Do you pace your longing,
time the yearning
so you don't run out of fennel crust
before the salmon, you before desire?

You cannot outlast your desire,
especially if you are walking
in a snow-sparkling field
wondering how her hand can be
so warm and small at the same time,
how it fits yours and then wriggles
into your pocket like a hot minnow.

It can't happen if she
breaks your disciplined line,
with her laugh almost silent,
but swims into your heart.

Or if you finally hook her, maybe
with song lines or rock group names:
"Echo & the Bunnymen."
I been thinking about my door bell
Why ain't you ringing it? Why
ain't you ringing it?

Or when you can't wait until the summer season.

REIFICATION

She tried to make it real for me,
holding my well stropped skin
against her clear soft roundness
pinching me alive,
making a dulled foil ready,
nicking me with quicksilver kisses;

but it could be no more real
to me than followed
that winter afternoon light:
the moon's ivory wide laser
shot miraculously into the carefully
closed house through the window
spot, worked clear
with warm mercury.

It could be no more real
to me than that accidental
meeting, brushing of cheeks
at the church corner, arms, breasts fitting,
as architectonically as her words:
If I sit next to you
will you hold me if I cry?
We were at the funeral of a friend,
and all that had gone before.

POMME DE TERRE

You have been everyone's sister
With your smiling-eyed, furrowed-browed
do-you-think? and *how-do-you* way?
How you touch on the arm and remember
our names, inserting one mid-sentence
like the treat in a lunch box
that we boys have been waiting for.

I waited for the repeal
of the laws of incest until
I could take it no longer,
waiting for your soft voice
and tender touch farther than the elbow,
and to have more of you
finding such pleasure in my eyes.

They will come after me now,
the other brothers, even sisters,
cousins, and Father.

I will not be forgiven
for introducing the serpent;
I will be told of all the other
fruit, the size of the garden,
with all the other
potential shameful dressers.

I will beg one last time:
not for the smooth, perfect fruit
left here, but please,
the ones so rough-skinned,
tart-sweet, forbidden for our own good;
for I am a damned man.

AFTER THE O'S

Oh, her mouth makes a pretty little circle,
I didn't really want to go out with you
again; I mean, you could see
we were just rebounding back,
but it's all right.

We walk like old friends
in the Renaissance or brothers
in my fraternity ritual, "two by two,
with arms locked firm and tight,"
except that we are old lovers, now finished.

We walk our favorite summer streets,
peering in the big house windows,
still open for fall; frankly snooping,
maybe for a shared old painting, silver,
or secret that holds that circle together.

I dressed in her favorite of my shirts
and took her for her favorite tappas,
which I don't like, and,
chaste, to her door.

She was as funny as ever,
telling of how she won
a childhood swimming competition
just trying not to drown.

THE GARDEN OF LOST GIRLFRIENDS

my ex told me as another old lover
breezed out the gate

We were at a poetry progressive
garden party: poem, appreciate garden,
poem, flowers, you know,
as long as human concentration
or, I feared, nature could hold out.

The evening shade was closing in
when that other old love stormed through
the gate. I thought I could save her
earlier, when the bees came after her
and I offered to change seats,
and what? Pretend I wasn't afraid?
Take the stings myself?

My commentator, garden-namer
said I should learn from all this.
I looked chastened,
but she was having none of it.

Like the keepers tell us of
those bees that won't
come back to the hives,
won't appreciate their slot combs
to work and give honey.

Inexplicably, they'd
rather just fly homeless
until they die. And we,
of hunger?

YES, I WILL MAYBE TAKE YOU BACK

if we can think of this
as an aberration, a lapse,
as two friends who will always be friends,
who stay together even
after a drunken argument.

But after that, I will take you
back only on a series
of conditions
that will be very hard,
but not impossible,
to meet—well, only if
you can hear the sub-text,
see the quiet.

But I prefer to take
you back after that,
when I can
shrink you to become
as a small, heated seed that
I will grow in my womb,
as bitter as tamarind.

MOMENTO MORI

Lost my soul
lost my locket
with my husband's remains
If found call 412-555-5899.

I wondered at the furnace of love
that can fire a locket of burnt kisses,
sworn commitments, and jealousies,
all shut around a neck.

Heat that can choke out fear
of death: to hold at the throat
with the hellish grit,
ashes of love.

I sometimes don't feel close enough
to anyone, my love, to give
even a posy necklace of a devotion
that it might not outlast.

I wish, my sweet, that we could
find such love, press it so close
between us, we would fire again,
to more than a dusty frosting
on loyal throats.

IV

What kind of people like to tell other people what to do?
A philosopher in defense of anarchy

If I'm killed, we've lost.
A friend during the Vietnam War

WOUNDED YEAR

This fall, the maples bleed
into deep November,
stain the dun landscape
with crimson markers.
Raccoons and possums, frantic,
but clumsy slow, litter the road side,
dead. Their arms reach out
as if for slipped-away dance partners.
I have this photo:
a Sicilian wedding sheet, a smeared
red flag, hung in a Palermo window
by some proud couple, reminding me
that even the innocent cut the bargain
that we will live the life
out of each other.

HAITI WELL

I have seen that sun that outs
everything about everyone,
that makes you hide in incendiary
colors in paintings that defy.
So unschooled brilliant,
they are the bricks of dreams.
I've heard the voodoo talk
maybe glimpsed cut-up chickens
in huts with three people,
always three, always believing,
scared to a trinity of resignation,
maybe understanding.

The sweat-terrified tourists
avoiding, then begging, protection,
in those days calling
the Ton Ton Macout;
if it's not Tuesday,
someone will be beaten like a drum.

Begging-poverty everywhere.
Do we know we had a hand
and hearts capable of not stopping it,
as sly and greedy as any Baby Doc's.

HAITI ILL

I'm from Pittsburgh where
we need the doors for closing
out the winter to say nothing
of the occasional robber, maybe drug addict.

We don't need those doors
for stretchers or make-
shift huts in the street
or make-shift coffins for
so many of maybe the luckiest Haitians.

Aside from shutting out the bad,
Pittsburghers need those doors most
to open and invite, like the sisters did,
who ran the orphanage and would not
run from or leave their children.
Imagine, two twenty-somethings facing
down a government. And we've opened
to let out a fine doctor who runs the hospital
his father founded, for many,
more, and too many Haitians

But it has been a long winter
and maybe we are afraid of losing
all the heat, but before we close,
let's at least unclasp the locks.

V2

Hitler put all his faith
into the V2 rocket,
the first to be used in warfare.

Eyes burning, he said
he wanted to annihilate.
V, not for victory, but vengeance.

So easy to see his stupidity,
meanness, hatred, trying to wipe out
the Jews, Gypsies, Slavs, 50 million,
including two of my uncles.

And my son learned in LA
that the sweet little bodega,
Mexican or Asian, is a myth.

I was recently remembering
that I arranged an abortion
for a woman I hardly knew.
And voted for a war
for which maybe we all
should go to Nuremberg.

This is not the story of a surely
aimed missile. Rather, of a circling vulture,
the remedy for which is always
too late, too wrong; like the supplies
to surrounded German troops at Stalingrad:
one plane filled with black pepper
and 12 cases of condoms.

RICHARD NIXON AND ME

There were terrible storms across Brazil
the TV weatherman said, and Richard Nixon's
Press Secretary said that the President's statement
was no longer operative, and my room mate
said *you don't have to be a weatherman* . . . .

just before we moved out
in the middle of the night
to avoid the rent.
We weren't the real crooks;
we might be drafted.

I am now in Rio,
and the warmth is forgiving.
I eat enough for a favela family
of four and throw away
enough for three more.

I imagine myself a Warsaw freedom fighter
not a Waffen SS Colonel in late 1945,
checking the plane schedules
from Berlin to here.

MAN LIVES SOME BY BREAD

I know an Internet address
to buy a Spanish ham,
and while I watch starvation
bloat the belly of a rail-thin boy
I wonder how I

eat so much and care so little
for those whose voices
outran their food
in this brutal interface of man's
bloody corrida with man.

RELIGION IS A TERRIBLE THING

I
Rabbi Lev, they say, tamed the Golem,
the inchoate earth man who terrorized
Prague until the rabbi taught him
to be good and protect the children,

until the golem thought he got
the word of God in his mouth
when Rabbi Lev wasn't there.
The golem returned to his unformed state,
went berserk, and nearly undid all his good.

II
Three times in my life,
I have had the word
of God in my mouth:

when I moved from a Catholic school
to a Protestant school,
I got into religious arguments
trying to help the nicest,
most foolish people.

The second time, god
told me—and I told you,
god didn't exist.

The third time you probably read about.
The federal government was involved.
My lawyers told me not to talk about it.

III
After Jonestown I just had
to go to church. What could
even that brilliant priest,
say about the Kool-Aid communion?
I remember his first words:

Religion is a terrible thing:
thinking about God is hot and prickly,
filled with righteous indignation, and controlling. . .

when Rabbi Lev is so hard to hear.

ST. VITUS REDUX

When I am in Prague I always go
to St. Vitus for Sunday high mass.
I go about as little as Kafka left his relentless home.

I sit next to the penitent man
kneeling in the aisle.
How great can his sin be?

I feel the intimacy of the priest's finger
placing the host trembling on my tongue,
the body of Christ.

The distant red stained glass window
looks like contact prints from Hell,
fire bleeding across the aisle.

Outside, so many carefully tended
flowers and trees, mulched by torn
out fingernails, blood, bones, and brains

as Hapsburg, Hitler, and Stalin
brought order to the chaos
of peace and then of each other.

Throwing people out windows
is a political tool here. One man
fell, saved, into a pile of manure.

But I am not here for them.
Like the man in the aisle next to me
on his knees, I pray from want:

out of this blitzkrieg rage
of too little winning, few things,
no even loves with women.

I face for a moment,
blessed cowardice, in this holy
emergency room, this cathedral.

RAIN QUEEN

The Queen of the Rain has died.
Modjadji V will no longer send
the cloudbursts that kept the mighty tribes
so in awe, except for their gifts during droughts.

The Zulu and Swazi left the Queen
and her Lobedu people alone in the mists
of the Drakensburg Mountains, where Modjadji
provided rain enough for ferns and bananas.

It is rumored that, like the queens before,
her body will lie under poured water for weeks
to create the rain potion and legend that made
deKlerk, Botha, and even Mandela wait.

All over Johannesburg that week, unseasonable
rains came down though her heart.

ANNOUNCING NOVEMBER

The leaf rot is so piquant
it could be the licorice
that Hemingway once said
was every longed-for taste.

Trees are so artfully placed
they could be by Turner,
light, just so in the middle distance,
to suggest the false mercy of storms.

Shadows entice from too far
to follow, yet close enough,
in a head-turn twist,
to be a swift bear hiding.

A tree limb, oddly red,
so precisely torn
as to be a lover's violation,
the wind a careless nurse.

In the park entrance,
two ancient women leer,
as if sharing a secret
from some first unholy annunciation.

V

Drum Man, street car, foot slipped, there you are.
Buddy Holly and the Crickets

Sometimes, God is there so suddenly.
Tennessee Williams

ELEVATOR

. . . for immortality is but ubiquity in time. . . .
                                        Herman Melville, *Moby Dick*

My hands still tremble
sometimes at the drop
of a voice, Dad's disapproval
Not To dialect.

I am in the port of Svakia, Crete,
alone at a table across
from the local toughs,
like my high school gang.

"Keep away from the moving wall"
the sign on the old Greek elevator
says, when it's perfectly clear,
not the wall, but we
are moving.

I know, for now I am my father
sitting worried in fourth grade
openly cheating because, he said, the test
was unfair. Or was his father?

He was liberated by France
and its lovely wine
and Canada's whiskey,
which he doted on for years.
I am for sweet honeyed yogurt in Greece
rather than the liquor in
my father's house in Pittsburgh
as dark as the Monongahela.

But I still shake before I leave
the homestead, even on this trip
to Greece, worry he will
lose the tickets, as when I was 12.
He won't be the smartest
in his Harvard class, heart
shaking in the maroon.

I become the tough boys escaping
their fathers in long draughts
and sweet sucks of tobacco,
hard, quick fights.

I now look up from the mirror
of the computer screen
to the wall mirror above:
I look so like my father;
I am so writing his poems.

We are all together in this elevator,
if standing only on spread
trembling legs, rising and falling.

THE HAWK OF SOUTH JERSEY

I saw him first in a Quasimodo getup,
as he slipped out the Delt house back door,
the cape, distorted by belted pillow prosthesis
humpback, hood well over his face.
He told me the story later: *they started*
chasing me; I climbed under a car
but my hump caught. They threw things
at me. I wanted to know
some of what he went through.

Later, we met in Dutch's Tavern
as editors planning the literary magazine,
the beers showing up, disappearing
as if vaporized.

One of us said *I always wait*
for the other person to quit.

He taught me about Shostakovich and Wagner
about Lenny Bruce and Joseph Heller
and, slapping his haunches, what aged beef
to order in Mercanti's Blue Room in Philadelphia.

I looked out for him through
that affair with the crazy pregnant woman,
stealing for her rent and the drugs.
We sat drunk, 5 A.M. in June in Philadelphia
unable for the fifth day to drive ourselves to the Jersey line.

Sundays at the Young Republican Club,
Bloody Marys to beer, 10 a.m. to midnight,
playing car tag with real cars,
stealing cars, slowly, one beer at a time,
gambling them away.

Taking dope, smuggling dope,
check fraud. "Cash" I called him.
What do you mean "no money"
gotta lotta checks, lotta ink;
lotta money.

I have lost him now.
Thirty years of recovery and twenty
of therapy taught me to divorce:
to be only me.
I am alive with family and friends,
sober; nice, they tell me,
responsible as hell.

But I miss that antic tower
when we were stuck, deformed,
occasionally able to fly out
past the cathedral gargoyles
and see so much of little known Paris.

HEMISPHERES

It was winter in Argentina
and everyone in Buenos Aires was coughing.
On La Rocha Street, it was
cold, even when touching
on the whores' couch,
those two with their tattoos:
the charming roses could bloom forever,
one small bud on the shoulder down
and one with a thorn up, on the thigh.

*

Back in Appalachia's late fall
my love takes us to concerts.
At night, her breasts above me,
she explains the music,
as she explained her forest's last colors.

When I don't get it,
her face comes close, like my doctor's,
who, when I asked about the origin
of a recurring fungus, insisted.
It's inside you.

THE BELLS OF RHYMNEY

I got my father's desk back
today, and I'm calling
in my markers for the rest:
redone, maple sweet with glass piece
reflecting to me all those memories
of the house I was raised in,
they called a home.

In an easy way
my family did not like me,
and we were even there.
But much of the money
now not in this desk was given me,
to keep me moving: in taxis,
at drinks in shady bars, and quietly,
with the girls on the Hill.

My parents did take me on vacations
that don't need refinished:
the white-capped New Jersey sea;
hot beach sand to lie on and inside my suit,
sweetly painful as that girl's first touches.

Surely, in one of the drawers is my mother's slam
shut of my brother and my brother's later punch
to my father, honest, right in the center support.
Almost knocked him out, me too.

In the top right locking drawer,
I can still find a pack of guitar strings
I kept for my friend who died too young.
I remember when we all stood outside that house
listening at midnight to him play his 12-string
and sing "The Bells of Rhumney,"

a song of desperate coal miners feeling
the anthracite walls become their prisons;
about the treachery of their masters
who were not minders;
also of children, stolen from, starved.

Oh, what will you give me,
say the sad bells of Rhymney.

Sad though it was,
the song settled in that fall
around the neighborhood trees and houses,
like a healing tonic.

The singer is long dead.
His tombstone says:
If you can read this,
you're standing on me.

WHERE'S MY SON, THE MUSICIAN?

You know the guy the musicians all yell at:
"Turn up the goddamn sound?"
Well, that's not me;
I'm the guy next to that guy.

Wheel of Fortune,
top row, right, that's me
usher near the doors,
cheesy red blazer.

I hear you say, John,
where you are,
but hard as I look
you are not there.

Maybe I find you somewhere else:
behind a Sunday morning
memory of bacon and bluegrass,
as I then tried to find us both

in the heartland of your rich heritage:
Mac Martin singing "Jimmy Brown;"
the University Chapel sermons
explaining why our ancestors can be
so kind, pious, dumb, and drunk.

I remember being next to you
and the trains going by Westinghouse park,
watching CSX, Lake Erie, Southern,
counting car by car, by father, by son.

Later, you found your own road
resonant with string basses,
lyric questions, and fair play.

I see you traveling that line,
not next to doors or sound engineers,
but alone: hard and well,
bright, unafraid, and swift.
I ache to give you a road map
that you are already drawing.

So I can only give you some
of my favorite bluegrass train song:
Jay Gould's daughter said before she died,
"Papa, fix the doors so the bums can't ride;
if ride they must, let them ride the rods;
let them put their trust in the hands of God."
As I must when you leave me.

MAGIC

The careless autumn day seemed to be
dropping its beauty thoughtlessly.
My nieces and nephews drift
toward their parents' porch,
children to be put in night home flight.

Stained and torn, they try to smuggle
past me, the border guard
of what remains their homeland.
So stunned with their own wizardry,
they almost forget Checkpoint Respect.

Finally, they turn themselves in:
young squires and ladies captured
before a foreign power, polite,
but looking past me for the coming night.

I hold a play-bruised niece and nephew,
tender in their trust of kinship,
angel wings up at the ghostly moon,
and I pledge a promise

softly for such a distance,
toward a brother's hardening grave:
blood passes as child's play.

PICTURE WINDOW

Don't be fooled by this smile.
I am closing in on my death day sure.
And have used up my drug taking
and luck a long time ago.
My only life now, out that window.

I am pleased to see
Nature as big an actor as I am.
So cool a being on the outside
but working so hard beneath,
above, everywhere hidden.

I see now that the lead goose is not just posing
for my postcard. Films shows him and the remaining V
reaching, straining for position, mating, and home,
idyllic momentarily as much the duck's serene sail
belies her frantic treadmill paddle beneath.

Why should I think those beautiful leaves' deaths
are any more pretty to them than my father's
choking, sputtering last hopeless,
breaths. They all died
as sure as a catheter stab. All unified
in a plentiful harvest of destruction.

Our loss, chaos, not even in season:
none of the order for which a little boy pleaded
at that very pond to the left there,
balancing in the geese feces and duck dung,
feeding bread, but backing away
from the charging and battling geese,

fearfully crying: *now is not the fighting time, geese.*
Now's the eating time.

SHAME

There are three things
I cannot think about
without closing out
all the world's light:

the way I stood on top
of my dormitory drunk,
all sweat and spinal shriveling,
defying the windy air
and lucky life God gave me.

And the time I called
a friend *nigger*
to prove I wasn't afraid
of the word or him
or loss of him
who was the harpsichord
of my life that year.

And the time at twelve
I bent my friend's arm so far,
elbow flat, over my shoulder
to flip him away — —from what?
his father's incessant company?
his mother's delicious pies?
I came so close to breaking
his atom structure,
my heart nearly explodes.

Nothing really happened.
My friend is a successful
lawyer with that arm writing writs
and checks, justly making
the high-rise suits pay
for the storefront coatless,
all in sunny Phoenix.

I never broke a back or leg.
The building still stands,
capped by my sixth-floor room
and empty ledge.

That black man graduated,
nice enough to me,
and joined my other fears,
shuttering out the bright universe
with dark slats of deepest bone.

WHEN FINISHING THAT EXCELLENT VINDELOO LAMB, I AM UNAWARE OF THE MOST SUBTLE TASTE

As Heisenberg taught us,
we overlook the weight of our
own thumb in a rush for
the final perfect Nano grams.

I am unaware of the finest filings
of rage toward the shortest slight,
that you pass off as nothing, until,
I meticulously strain it over and over.

Not so much for the faintest film
of each tooth's pure porcelain
that so precisely forks through meat,
leaving only miniscule tang,

but for the precious drops
of bile that intravenously feed
all of me as, glacially, relentlessly,
I consume my own teeth.

SERMON

Before the East End clean up,
parts of Pittsburgh were so arched
by fragile towering trees, old streets
in winter were crumbling wood cathedrals.

Then, more artists than rich people
lived on Ellsworth Avenue in condemned
if not officially marked houses.
And drank wine and frightened each other.

I saw a boy, perhaps 17, at an artists' party
caught up with attractive fast talking men,
bitterly laughing sotto voce
at a beautiful dark haired folk singer.
I heard the term *mush mouth.*

I thought she sang beautifully,
but her eyes followed like lasers
the boy's unsteady walk around,
even as he went into a back room
with a gifted nickel bag.

Drunk, as usual, I went outside
for some air and fell asleep in my car.
I awoke at 3:00 and drove home,
but as I passed the Presbyterian Church
I saw the boy kneeling
in the snow in front.

I wanted to ask him if he needed a ride,
for I needed some human communion.
But for the first time I saw that
God was not finished yet.

SHROUDED

—After the wood sculpture, "Shrouded"

ascended right out of the artist's box—
hooded, indefinite of expression,
bold in sadness of outline—
and began staring at me,
polished wood ring to my eye,
knot to back, I started to see
the axe split between
virgin birth and death:
begging touch to its smooth finish,
burl pieta, lost of Christ.

Oh, but she sees:
watching my poem's dancing
or cutting corners; or when I'm lying
satiated in bed with another guest
in the pitch, no longer talking;
she stares! Projects?
That left foot space near my heel,
dead of feeling for some time,
is now just a little limb spore of me,
but growing slowly, relentlessly as an oak.

HOW WILL I DIE?

A Hopeful Prayer

You may see me
as blurry, ashen, aching,
breaking apart in your
horror at my jarring pain.

But that will not be me,
bedded to be boxed and lillied,
an apparition in the vacant corner
of my redoubtable couch.

How will I die?
I will drive a navy blue coupe
into the deep green summer,
and be carried south,

through mountains of Carolina pines
until my deep blue ride,
and God's golden, moving summer
are indistinguishable:

violet cornflower gaining millennium speed;
at first, as blurry, refracted
as in your frightened eyes.
Then clearly, only one forest green.